HOW TO DEV

The immateri memory records planet can be 'rea the hand or pressed to the forehead. This book reveals the techniques to employ.

*By the same author*

APPRENTICED TO MAGIC
HOW TO DEVELOP CLAIRVOYANCE
HOW TO READ THE AURA
INTRODUCTION TO TELEPATHY
MAGIC AND THE QABALAH
MAGIC: ITS RITUAL POWER AND PURPOSE
THE MAGICIAN: HIS TRAINING AND WORK

# HOW TO DEVELOP PSYCHOMETRY

*by*

W.E. Butler

THE AQUARIAN PRESS
Wellingborough, Northamptonshire

First published 1971
Third Impression 1975
Second Edition, revised and reset, 1979
Second Impression 1983





ISBN 0 85030 180 7 (UK)
ISBN 0 87728 440 7 (USA)

Printed and bound in Great Britain by
Richard Clay (The Chaucer Press) Ltd.,
Bungay, Suffolk

# CONTENTS

## CHAPTER ONE

# A TALE TO UNFOLD

You must often have heard people say, when looking at some object of historical interest, 'What a tale it could unfold, if it could only speak'. Those of us who have practical knowledge of what is popularly known as E.S.P. (short for Extra-Sensory-Perception) know from our own experience that this saying is true. The historic article, indeed every article, not only has a tale to tell, but it is already telling it constantly, in the same way, to use an analogy, that the magnetic tape of a tape-recorder has imprinted upon it words or music which, under suitable conditions, may be heard again and again as they are reproduced by the machine.

It is true that there is no instrument, electrical or otherwise, which can reproduce for us the sights and sounds, the emotions passions and thoughts which have been recorded upon material objects. Certain people, however, appear to have a kind of 'sixth sense' which enables them to pick up these hidden vibrations and impressions, and bring them into their waking consciousness. Such people are called 'psychometrists'.

The word is derived from two Greek words, *psyche*, meaning 'the soul', and *metron*, signifying a 'measure'. So by this definition, psychometry is the power to measure and interpret 'the soul of things'.

**Professor Denton**

This name was given to the faculty by an American Professor of Geology in the nineteenth century. Professor Denton carried out an exhaustive series of tests with the aid of his sister, Mrs Ann Denton Cridge. He found that if she held a geological specimen to her forehead, even though it was carefully wrapped up, so that its nature could not be guessed at through its appearance, she was able to obtain, through vivid pictures which arose 'in her mind's eye', some knowledge of the past history of the particular specimen being tested.

Denton wrote a most interesting book, *The Soul of Things*, dealing with the psychometric faculty, and gives therein some fine examples of the accuracy of the visions of his sister. Perhaps at the present time we may feel that he did not allow for the possibility of telepathy between himself and his sister, and because of this the value of some of the evidence for a supernormal faculty is somewhat weakened. However, this applies to only a small part of his researches.

Denton had been drawn to the study of this strange faculty by reports given by a certain Dr Rhodes Buchanan, who experimented with some of his students by getting them to hold phials containing powerful drugs. He found that some of them, when handling phials distinguished only by a numbered label, began to experience the physical reactions which would have been produced in them by an actual dose of the drug in question.

## Metallic Taste

Buchanan himself had been started off along this particular trail by the chance information that, during the American Civil War, a certain General Palk had found that if he touched anything metallic, even in the dark, he experienced a curious metallic taste in his mouth.

Through the researches of Denton the word 'psychometry' was first coined, but since that time the word has come to bear a secondary meaning, and it is in this secondary sense that it is now used by psychologists. The dictionary definition of the word gives both meanings. It reads: 'The measurement of the duration of the mental processes used in psycho-analysis and intelligence testing. Also, the occult faculty of divining, by touching an object, the character, personal qualities, etc., of another person who has handled it.'

It is somewhat amusing to note how eagerly the psychologists, as a body, try to dissociate themselves from the primary meaning of the word as coined by Denton, and attempt to convince the public that the word belongs to them, and has no possible connection with the firm next door: the 'occultists'!

## A Psychometrist at Work

Having briefly dealt with the modern rediscovery of this psychic faculty (it was well known in various parts of the world in past centuries) let us now watch, in imagination, a psychometrist at work.

There are 'psychometry meetings', so-called, where a professional psychometrist deals with a number of articles brought by members of the audience. As a rule, the objects are placed in separate compartments on a tray, in order, it is said, to prevent the influences of one article affecting others near it. This, as we know from practical experience, is not always a complete safeguard against mixed influences.

In this connection, a story from the beginnings of modern psychometric experimentation may be of interest. A certain lady who had been told of this strange new power, had gone to bed one night, and was lying awake thinking about psychometry as it had been described to her. Suddenly she determined to make a practical test to see if there was anything in the idea. So getting out of bed in the dark she went downstairs without a light and from her writing desk chose at random a letter from a collection of letters which she kept in chronological order in one of the desk drawers.

She duly held the letter to her forehead and tried to 'see' something about the person who had written it, and was rewarded by finding a flood of impressions coming to her mind. These impressions built up the character and general outlook of one man, a very strong-willed and powerful person. Full of excitement at this proof of the reality of this strange power, she went back to bed without even attempting to see if her impressions were correct; she felt so sure that they were.

**Astonishment and Disillusionment**

Waking in the morning, she remembered her midnight psychometric experiment, and eagerly looked at the letter which she had brought up with her and which now lay on the table beside her bed. To her great astonishment and disillusionment, the character of the writer of the letter in no way whatsoever resembled that which she had felt in her experiment.

Full of gloom she went down to replace the letter in its correct position in the drawer. As she did so, she glanced at the letter which lay next to it in the bundle, and saw, with delight, that all that she had felt when attempting to psychometrize the letter she had chosen was to be found in the character of the writer of this one which had been lying next to it. The strong virile character had impressed itself not only on the actual letter, but also upon the weak influence of the letter next to it.

**An Imaginary Reading**

Returning to our psychometric readings, we

see that the psychometrist takes an article and either holds it in his hand or presses it to his forehead, and proceeds to describe that which he feels and 'sees' as he comes into psychic contact with it. Here is an imaginary reading, based upon our own experience with a good psychometrist:

'I see before me a wide expanse of water – I think it is the sea. Yes, I feel it is the Atlantic ocean. I am standing on the deck of a ship – it seems to be a wooden ship – it is a warship of some kind, for I see guns – muzzle-loading guns of Nelson's time or thereabouts. The sea appears to be a deep blue and is very calm, and the sunlight is strong. In the distance there is a low coast-line, and I see, nestling in the low hills which rise behind the sand dunes of the coast, a town of white-walled buildings. My attention is drawn to a man who is evidently the captain of this ship. He is dressed in the uniform of an officer in the Royal Navy of Nelson's time. I feel that some of the trees on the hills are olive trees, and I think this must be either Spain or Portugal. The ship appears to be taking part in blockading this seaport town.

**Prominent Churchman**

'Now I am looking at a ring – a gold ring with a large amethyst set in it – it is this same ring which I am now holding – I feel a sense of power and authority in connection with this. Why, it belongs to this officer, but it takes me back very many years before this time. I seem to be in Italy – at least that is the impression I get – and I feel that the original owner of this ring lived in Italy and was a prominent Churchman of his time – I sense he was a bishop or some such dignitary – there is a sound as of Latin being chanted, and I feel that this ring goes back to the time of the Renaissance.

'This must have been handed down to the captain as an heirloom and has in the same way been passed down to its present possessor.

'Now I want to come to the person who gave in this ring for a reading. You are at present at the parting of the ways, and you are finding it very difficult indeed to decide which path to choose – they seem equally compelling. I feel, however, that within a short time – and this will be measured in days, not weeks, the matter will become clear to you and the way forward be opened up. Do not make any sudden move until this clear indication of the correct line to take presents itself.'

**Sea Captain**

The recipient of this message confirms that the ring did in fact belong to one of Nelson's sea captains, an ancestor of his, and it was at one time owned by one of the great Catholic bishops of the Renaissance period. He also agrees that he is indeed approaching a crisis in his material affairs, and cannot make up his mind as to which will be the correct course to follow.

This is a typical psychometric reading of the better type. Some such readings are much better, some very much worse, but this gives a fair idea of what may be expected.

You will notice that there are three definite levels in this particular reading. There is the description of the original owner of the ring and his general surroundings, there is the description of the sea captain and *his* general conditions, and finally there is a statement made concerning the present owner of the article.

The first level we may term its 'primary record', the second its secondary level, the level concerning the present and future conditions of the owner of the ring being what may be described as the tertiary level. These three levels will be found, in varying proportions, in all psychometric readings.

## The Source of Knowledge

The question arises, how has the psychometrist obtained his knowledge? In the majority of cases we can rule out collusion between the psychometrist and the owner of the article concerned. Where such collusion does happen, it is soon detected and dealt with. We are left with a very considerable body of statements which have to be explained in some other way.

A detached study of the matter usually

reveals the presence of much which is not in any way evidential. It is due to the psychological fact that the 'level of acceptance', if we may so call it, varies considerably from one person to another. There are those whose critical faculty is slight, and such people will accept as evidence much that more critical people would not regard as being in any way evidential. So what we may term the 'credibility factor' has to be taken into account when judging the statements made.

We would point out, however, that often what appears to be a triviality may have a real significance for the person concerned, and it is sometimes these very trivialities which provide conclusive proof of the accuracy of the statements made by the psychometrist.

**Evidential Statements**

When, however, we have discounted those vague general statements which are obviously non-evidential, but are what we might describe as verbal 'padding', we are left with positive and detailed statements which are truly evidential, and which cannot be explained away by any theories of fraud or wishful thinking. So we are back to our question of how these evidential statements came into the mind of the psychometrist. It was obviously not through the ordinary five senses.

One answer, of course, is that the

knowledge was received telepathically from the mind of the owner of the article which was being psychometrized. This may be so in some instances, but we feel that by invoking the telepathic explanation, we are simply substituting one form of extra-sensory-perception for another, and in many cases the information simply does not exist within the mind of any living person.

The sceptic is therefore often driven to formulating a 'pool of knowledge', a 'cosmic memory', from which, it is alleged, the psychometrist draws his information. It is an attractive theory, and, quite apart from the way in which it is sometimes employed against the claims of the spiritualists, it does fit in with the results of psychometrical practice.

It will be useful, perhaps, to take a look at this idea of a pool of knowledge upon which we may draw under certain conditions.

Those who are acquainted with the work of the late Dr C.G. Jung will remember that he put forward in his writings the idea of what he called the 'Collective Unconscious', which lies behind the normal individual consciousness with which we are all familiar. Each person, in the depths of his subconscious nature, is linked up directly with this collective *un*conscious. Because of this we may, under certain circumstances, bring through into the waking consciousness some of the knowledge which lies in those hidden realms of the mind.

## The Astral Light

This concept of the collective unconscious is one which is familiar to anyone who has studied the teachings of what is usually called occultism. By them the collective unconscious is known as 'the astral light' and it is held that the activities of this collective unconscious work through many varying degrees of an immaterial 'substance' which underlies all physical matter.

It is further held that this underlying substance not only contains the memory records, both conscious and subconscious, of all life upon the physical planet, but it is also the channel through which the all-embracing Consciousness of the Creator and Sustainer of this universe holds all manifestation, on all levels of existence, within Its power and control.

## The Akashic Records

In the East, the divine life and consciousness is said to work in and through what is known as 'Akasha', and for this reason we find the term 'The Akashic Records' employed to refer to this 'cosmic memory'. This, is, of course, only a very rough outline of a very intricate system of philosophy, but it may serve to explain the use of the term 'The Akashic Records'.

It is further taught that these Akashic Records are reflected at varying levels in the Astral Light, and are liable to suffer some distortion when near to the emotional and mental currents which surge through the collective unconscious of the planet.

So we have the concept of an all-embracing mind and consciousness not far removed from earth-life and its struggles, but actually immanent within it as well as remaining in Its Fullness above and beyond all manifestation.

It is also held that by virtue of his own innate divinity, man may become, in varying degree, *en rapport* with that divine consciousness, and in proportion as he does this, he is able to make contact with that cosmic memory, of which his own personal memory is but a fractional part.

### Soul of the World

With James and Fechner and many other philosophers, the occultists also hold that this planet is not a mere inert ball of mineral matter swinging through the heavens, but is the 'body' or vehicle of a mighty but simple life, and because of this it possesses its own memory of all that has happened upon it.

Every particle of matter is, by this hypothesis, understood to be a means whereby the *Anima Mundi*, the Soul of the World, may be contacted.

### The Reflecting Ether

So we come to the simple definition of Denton and his co-workers, that in psychometry we are making contact with and reading in the indelible memory of the soul of things. Incidentally, the occultists say that this planetary memory is recorded in what they term the 'reflecting ether' of the planet. This reflecting ether not only holds the planetary memory, but also reflects clearly or otherwise, according to circumstances, the fore-knowledge of the Divine Mind which is ever in the true Akashic Records.

Thus, through the reflecting ether, some glimpses of futurity, some 'shadows cast before' may be obtained by the psychometrist, but such foretelling of the future will depend for its accuracy upon how clearly those reflections of the Divine Mind are being mirrored in the depths of the memory of the *Anima Mundi*.

In passing we may suggest that it was the knowledge of the existence of this universal memory which was symbolized by the records which were read, according to the old Egyptian belief, when the discarnate soul was brought to the judgement of the gods, and some of this Egyptian symbolism may have been brought over into Christianity in the images of the book of Revelations, where it is said that the 'books were opened' and the dead were judged.

## Developing the Faculty

Having given you something of the theories and hypotheses which have been put forward to explain the phenomena of psychometry, we would point out that, interesting and instructive though such ideas may be, it is as well if we get 'down to earth' and concentrate upon developing the faculty; one can always argue about the metaphysics of it at a later date when personal practical experience has been gained.

It is not necessary that you should hold any particular theory about psychometry; you can just develop the faculty and use it without accepting any one theory, just as one can see without any expert knowledge of optics. Once you have developed the psychometric faculty you can use it, as indeed you can use *all* faculties, both physical and super-physical, for whatever purpose appeals to you.

Remember, however, that increased ability brings with it increased responsibility to use it in the right way, and here, of course, you come up against the moral aspect of such development. Concerning this we shall have more to say later in this book.

CHAPTER TWO

# CONCERNING PSYCHIC GIFTS

An idea has grown up that psychic faculties, such as clairvoyance, clairaudience, psychometry and so on, are peculiar 'gifts' bestowed by nature on certain individuals, and are not faculties possessed by all mankind. This belief has three aspects. First of all, there is the old 'pagan' idea of the 'gods' showering gifts upon men. More particularly, since it was thought that such psychic qualities enabled some kind of link to be made between the gods and their worshippers, the psychic qualities, above all others, were regarded in a special way, and around their use there gathered the 'numinous' atmosphere of religion.

At the heart of the primitive religions of mankind was to be found the idea of the 'oracle', the seer, the 'soothsayer', and behind the official exoteric religion of the day an 'inner' or 'esoteric' teaching and practice.

When Christianity began to emerge as a religion there arose various groups which are generally listed together as 'Gnostics', for they claimed to have *direct* personal *knowledge* of spiritual things. Many of those who had come over into Christianity from one or another of the old Mystery Faiths, felt that a great deal of their previous knowledge could be 'baptized into Christ' and many of them became influential teachers in the infant Church.

## Psychic Faculties

It is worth noting that in both the classical Mysteries and early Christian Gnosticism, the use of the psychic faculties did not imply any such communications with the 'spirits' of discarnate human beings as modern spiritualism envisages, but was concerned with contact with spiritual beings of various kinds.

When, by any mischance, what appeared to be a discarnate human being made itself felt, it was held that something had gone wrong, and steps were taken to prevent its recurrence. It is worth emphasizing the point that neither Egyptian 'Kerheb', Elusinean Hierophant, Neo-Platonic Theurgist nor Christian Gnostic sought communication with the 'dead' through mediumship, though all forms of psychic faculty were known to them.

This, of course, does not disprove the spiritualistic explanation, but as many spiritualists have claimed that such contact *must* have been made, and that only with *human* spirits, it is necessary to point out that although the possibility of such contact with the dead cannot be ruled out, those whom we have mentioned did not in any way regard it as the primary object of their psychic practices.

**St Paul**

In a well-known passage in one of his letters to his Corinthian converts, St Paul gives instructions to the small groups of Christians who met together for spiritual communion and prayer.

It must be kept in mind that the early 'Followers of the Way', as the Christians were first called, took the promise of their Lord and Master very seriously indeed. He had told them that He would send the Holy Spirit to them, to lead them, and they believed that the influence of this same Holy Spirit was to be found in all the gatherings of the faithful. It was, they said, a 'Spirit-filled Church'.

In the small groups gathered together for worship and communion, psychic phenomena manifested, just as they did many centuries later in the similar groups of the Society of Friends (more commonly known as the 'Quakers'.)

Here again, in the Quaker Meetings it is held to be the power and presence of the Spirit, rather than the efforts of the so-called 'dead', which produces them.

**Psychic Gifts**

Paul indeed says that the one and selfsame Spirit apportions to each person a particular 'gift' or 'charism', and here we find a link with the pagan and also the Jewish idea of the gods or God, giving gifts to men.

An unfortunate translation of the Greek

has made Paul refer to '*spiritual*' gifts, but the phrase is more correctly translated as 'psychic' gifts, i.e., appertaining to the soul or 'psyche', rather than to the spirit; to Paul, man was a trinity of body, soul and spirit.

So, from pagan antiquity, through the Christian ages up to the present time, these psychic faculties have been regarded as gifts from above, and this attitude of mind has also been applied to *all* the faculties of man. Thus, we speak of a gifted speaker, a gifted artist or a gifted musician. In all these cases we are using the thought forms of the past, and this is especially noticeable when we come to deal with the psychic faculties.

**Threshold of Waking Consciousness**

There is, however, another point of view, which is implicit in the teachings which form the basis of the philosophy of life of the present writer. This is, that the psychic faculties are present in all men, and, indeed in a latent fashion in all life, but in some cases they are working above the threshold of the normal waking consciousness, whereas in the majority they are *below* that threshold. How far they lie below that threshold determines whether it is worth the effort needed to bring them into conscious working activity. In some cases it simply would not be worthwhile.

Let us take an illustration from another of the 'gifts', that of music. There have been those who, at a very early age, showed an aptitude for the subject, and such a talent for musical composition and expression as to be regarded as musical prodigies. Music and its expression appear to be innate in them. Some of the great musical composers come into this category.

As an example of the other end of the scale, the present writer may be taken as an illustration. He has never, from earliest childhood, been able to sing in tune, being partly 'tone-deaf', and the mysteries of orchestral performance are as closed books to him.

During his early schooldays, he was given a book to read when the singing lesson was on, for not only could he not sing two notes in tune but no one within a fifty yard radius could sing either, if *he* tried! It is obvious that any time spent by him in musical training would be entirely wasted.

**Spontaneous Activity**

So it is with the psychic faculties. In some cases they seem to spring spontaneously into activity. In others, years of 'sitting for development' will fail to bring them into action. Most people, however, lie between these two extremes. They can develop or unfold such faculties, but the time needed to do this varies with each individual.

However, to unfold a faculty is one thing; to stabilize it and have it under one's control is quite another! It is here that so many would-be psychics fail the test. They make no attempt to discipline and train their psychic ability, and this very often springs from the mistaken idea of 'gifts' which we have already considered. We shall return to this whole question of stabilization, discipline and training later on in this book, but we felt we should just refer to it at this point.

We come now to the ethical point of view. As we have already pointed out, an unfortunate translation has connected these faculties with the idea of 'spirituality'. It is therefore worthwhile to consider what this term means, and how far it may be applied to these supernormal faculties which lie within each of us.

## Spirit and Matter

In the early Christian Church, there arose a curious 'heresy' or point of view (for that is what the word 'heresy' originally meant) which made a clear-cut division or 'dichotomy' between 'Spirit' and 'Matter'. The beginnings of this can be traced in some parts of the letters of St Paul, but it came into prominence in the teachings of a certain Manes, a Christian teacher who had adopted some of the ideas of the Persian religion of Zoroastrianism. Spirit and Matter were regarded as eternally opposed and Matter was held to be absolutely evil.

This heresy, though condemned by the great Councils of the Church, has never been entirely banished from Christendom, and has appeared in various guises again and again.

It was the basis of the Puritan streak which runs through the whole of Christian history, and it caused any natural and necessary reaction to licentious teaching and conduct to become badly emphasized and out of balance, resulting in a teaching and practice equally detrimental to the true development of the spirit of man.

**Faulty Translation**

Now, although those schools of thought which teach the use of the psychic faculty claim to have become free from 'orthodox' ideas, they are still apparently bound by this faulty translation of the New Testament concerning psychic gifts, and very many of their followers persist in regarding these faculties as *spiritual* gifts.

In so far as all man's powers and faculties are spiritual, in the true sense, for Matter is but one manifestation of Spirit, they are correct, *but* and this is a big 'but', if they do so regard *psychic* faculties as spiritual, then they must also regard man's *physical* faculties as equally spiritual, otherwise they fall into the Manichaean heresy.

Unfortunately, however, the error persists that the possession of a psychic faculty of necessity means that the person concerned is also a 'spiritual' person in the ethical and moral sense. Anyone who is acquainted at first hand with the world of psychism and allied subjects knows full well that this is not the case, yet the idea is strongly entrenched, and will no doubt be with us for a long time. As we have seen, it has a long history, and cannot be eliminated in five minutes.

The fact remains, that the possessor of psychic faculties and mediumistic abilities is not necessarily a person of high moral and spiritual character. Indeed, the reverse is very often the case.

### Telepathic Suggestions

We have already referred to the varying depths of the mind in which these psychic faculties may be latent. Let us now consider the case of one in whom these faculties are very near the surface of the subconscious mind, but are not within the conscious field of the waking self. They are, however, constantly acting in the subconscious levels, receiving impressions from the thoughts and emotions of others around them.

All these impressions are coming into their minds as suggestions, some good, and some bad, and are constantly altering the whole consciousness.

All men are linked together in this manner, no man is an island, as one poet has said, and, quite apart from our common subconscious base in what is known as the 'Collective Unconscious' of the race, we are ever surrounded by and immersed in a swirling sea of thought and emotion, through which flow rhythmic tides of energy, and to the content of this unseen sea we are ever responding, whether or not we are aware of it.

### Life of a Prostitute

So it often happens that a woman adopts the life of a prostitute not because she consciously chose such a path, but because of the effect upon her partially awakened psychic senses of the thoughts and emotions of others concerning her. Her very sensitivity has betrayed her.

If she was brought up with certain ideals of conduct in sexual matters, she may have resisted the combined pull of her natural instincts and the insidious suggestions which reached her through her hidden sensitivity. Then a time may have come when she was for the moment, 'off guard', and the instinctive urges and the telepathic suggestions combined to lose her emotional and ethical balance, and so she 'fell into sin'.

But the blame for that fall may well lie with someone who, with virtuous 'respectability' prejudged her, and, by the weight of this thought (itself very often the product of thwarted sexual urges) contributed to her downfall. 'Condemn not, that ye be not condemned' is a very sound injunction.

### A Code of Living

Because of this psychic interaction between ourselves and all around us, it is highly desirable that, if we would most truly be 'ourselves', we should consciously and deliberately construct for our daily life and work a code of living, a standard of ethics and morals, which will prevent us being at the mercy of these unseen but powerful influences which we are receiving from our environment.

We know the necessity of such codes of thought and conduct in the face of the visible and tangible temptations we meet in ordinary waking life. Even more so are such codes needed as a guard against these unseen and intangible subconscious temptations.

Having established such a code of living, we may safely attempt to bring into the conscious waking mind the impressions which are being received by way of these submerged psychic senses. When thus brought under our conscious control, they cease to be the hidden uncharted sources of some of our irresponsible thinking, and we begin to be less affected by the composite 'mob-mind' of those around.

We are in the course of obeying the rule which in ancient days was inscribed over the Temple of the Mysteries: *Gnothi seauton*, which simply means 'Know Thyself!' When the psychic impressions are thus brought into consciousness, it is possible to judge their value and to deal with them within the code of living which has been developed.

## Science of the Soul

The reader is in a position to make use of

them for his own true advancement in character, and, by being consciously aware of them he will no longer be at their mercy. He can observe the conditions which will allow them to work, and can also begin to assess their value to him in his life. If his mind is of the scientific type, then he may also be able to begin to spell out the alphabet of what is, in these modern times, a long forgotten science: a science of the soul.

It is true that in the present state of our modern knowledge regarding these faculties, their exercise partakes far more fully of *art*, rather than *science*, but as progress is made in understanding the laws which govern their manifestation, it will begin to be seen what a sublime science lies behind the workings of these supernormal faculties.

**Yoga Systems**

This science has never been entirely lost to mankind, though in the West it has apparently been obscured because of the type of civilization which has been built up here. In the East, however, it has persisted more openly in the various Yoga systems, fragments of which are being so assiduously peddled in the West at the present time. Much of this is a travesty of the true teaching.

In both the East and West, however, there are those who are the initiates and custodians of this Ageless Wisdom, and they stand ready to assist those in the Western world who, at this momentous point in the history of man, are engaged in research work in this field of the supernormal.

The faculty of psychometry is one of the most interesting and instructive of these paranormal powers, and if rightly used it can be of great value.

## Special Training

It is comparatively easy to acquire *some* ability to psychometrize without any special training, but it is far better, from every point of view, if some definite system of training is undergone by the would-be psychometrist. The faculty so trained is in every way superior to the untrained variety.

The training necessary for the development of the psychometric faculty can be divided into several techniques, and in the next chapter we will deal with these in some detail. However, before we pass on to that, we would like to explain what may have seemed to some of our readers an excessive use of the word 'faculty'. Most people who deal with these things would commonly refer to 'psychic *powers*', but we prefer to use the term 'faculty' as it is a more correct description of them. They are *receptive* faculties, not *expressed powers*.

# CHAPTER THREE

# PRELIMINARY TRAINING

We have already pointed out that it is quite possible to develop the power of psychometry without *any* training, as, of course was the case with the pioneers in the modern re-discovery of the faculty. Indeed, this holds good of all new discoveries or re-discoveries, for it is only by repeated experiment and classification of the results obtained that the underlying laws of the subject are formulated. It then becomes possible to devise a method of systematic training.

However, even when such a system of training has been evolved, it must always be kept in mind that the exercise of these psychic faculties, although based on a true scientific foundation, is also very much of an *art*, and any system of training must allow for the *personal* factors involved.

A similar state of affairs is to be found in the visual arts; a painter, for instance, may have a very exact mechanical technique of painting, but the real value of his work will lie in the personal element which he puts into his pictures. So it is with this psychic faculty of psychometry.

## The Rule of Natural Law

The reference to a 'scientific' basis to psychic practice may cause surprise to many of our readers, who have always understood that these things belonged to a 'supernatural' order of things, and were not therefore amenable to scientific law. However, those who have studied these matters most deeply are convinced that they are indeed subject to the rule of natural law.

It is necessary, perhaps, to point out that when we talk of the natural laws of the universe, we are really referring to what has been termed 'the predictable sequence of events observed over a long period' and not to the actual immutable cosmic law which is the very framework of this universe. In other words, it is *our concept* of the *true* natural law.

An example is to be found in the Newtonian hypotheses of gravity and light. Within certain limits these theories work well, and account for most of the observed facts, but there *are* facts which do not fit into their scheme, whereas the general hypothesis of Relativity, as formulated by Einstein, does cover them.

In the same way, the Victorian scientists, forming their hypotheses upon a purely material basis, were convinced that psychic manifestations had no part in the 'rational universe' of scientific thought.

## New Hypotheses

'There is no place in the universe for ghosts' declared one of them, and another declared, 'In matter I see the promise and potency of all life'.

We have made this digression in order to point out that the 'laws of nature' as expressed at any one time, may well be superseded by new hypotheses formulated at a later date. All are but theories, hypotheses, built up to express and explain certain facts. Behind them all is the immutable law of the universe, and the truth or falsity of any 'natural law hypothesis', depends upon how closely it approaches to that *true* law.

The annals of scientific history are crowded with examples of the relative accuracy of the theories evolved by scientific thinkers to account for the observed phenomena of nature.

*All* hypotheses and statements about natural law are conditioned by our understanding of the facts observed, our personal prejudices, both conscious and subconscious, and the scope and extent of our experience of the subject. This was not always understood by the Victorian scientists or, for that matter, by many scientists today.

A short time ago we heard a prominent psychologist declare that no amount of evidence would ever make him entertain the idea of the possibility of Extra-Sensory-Perception, since to admit such a possibility would destroy the basis of all modern teaching.

**Religious Thinkers**

A similar 'blockage' exists also in the minds of many religious thinkers, and this shows itself in the tendency to make a hard and fast division between things 'sacred' and things 'secular'. It is this mental outlook which has always tended to regard the psychic faculties as being 'supernatural'.

We do not subscribe to this belief, for in common with most of those who have worked along these lines, we hold the belief that the only 'supernatural' is the One Who is above all Nature because He is its Fount and Origin. We also believe that it is the Will and Purpose of this One which is the true law of the Universe.

### Super-Normal Manifestation

So all manifestation, on whatever plane of existence, comes under the natural laws, and should not be termed 'supernatural'. It is usual, therefore, to refer to the psychic faculties as 'super-normal'. It follows, then, that they come into the realm of scientific observation and method.

Equally, much of the testing and investigating which is carried out is anything but scientific, and its extremes at both ends of the mental scale show a similar pigheadedness and an unwillingness to follow the dictum of the great Victorian scientist, Huxley, who said that the true scientist must be prepared to 'sit down before Nature as a little child, and follow where she leads'.

In what we have written here in

connection with the training of the psychometric faculty we have tried to avoid the two extremes of intellectual aridity on the one hand and sentimental stupidity on the other.

## Example of an Inadequate Reading

You will remember that we gave a brief outline of a 'psychometry meeting', and we said that the 'reading' given by the psychometrist was one of the better type. We now want to portray a psychometric 'reading' of the poorer variety. You will notice that the statements made are quite evidential, and are recognized by the owner of the article. It is not in the information given, but in its presentation that the weakness lies.

Our psychometrist takes the article and says: 'I see a lot of water – there's a man here – I think it is the sea – the man has a queer uniform – I see quite a lot of trees, greyish-green leaves – I have a feeling of Church influence – incense – the trees are growing on low hills behind a town – are you in some doubt as to the best thing to do? – there are Italian influences connected with this article – the man is looking at something – have you been intending to go to Italy? – I get the idea of guns going off – were you in the War? – the man is wearing a sword, he seems to be in command of something – don't worry, the way will be made plain for you in a few days'.

## Selective Action

You will observe that this 'reading' contains most of the evidential facts given by the first psychometrist, but instead of being a coherent series of statements, it is a mass of jumbled fragments. How does this arise?

There are two main factors and one subsidiary one. First of all, it is a peculiarity of the psychic faculties that the information received through them comes into the mind as a solid block of knowledge, and this is then sorted out by the subconscious mind and projected into the waking consciousness in some kind of sequence.

Incidentally, this same kind of thing happens with ordinary physical vision. The eyes present the total picture they are receiving to the visual centre in the brain and this results in information being passed through the subconscious into the waking consciousness. Normally, there is a selective action which goes on in the subconsciousness, and it is this subconscious selective action which breaks up the block of visual impressions received and presents its parts in a particular pattern to the waking self.

The subconscious selective action is triggered off by several things. We may have been reading about a river in flood, and the damage it has caused, and then, in the course of the day we are in country conditions in which, amongst many other things, a river is seen. Almost invariably the first thing we shall notice about the countryside we are looking at will be the river, because our subconsciousness has been keyed to it by our reading earlier in the day.

## Psychological Bias

Or we may have a great antipathy to certain animals, cows, for example, and without consciously being aware of it, our first observation is that there are cows around! Here we come to the second factor in this matter of perception. A psychological bias has automatically built up in our subconsciousness, and all incoming impressions from any of the senses are affected by it on their way through to the conscious levels of the mind.

If we know what bias we have in any direction, we are able to consciously compensate for it, but if we are unaware of even having such a mental twist, then it is liable to affect our judgement of what we receive through our senses. Particularly is this the case when we have to assess and record what we saw or heard.

This is well known in police and legal circles. Two witnesses of the same accident, standing at the time in almost the same place, will give two honest, straightforward accounts of what happened, and these two reports will virtually contradict each other!

This imperfect selection of impressions is obvious in some of the 'descriptions' given by clairvoyants and psychometrists, and is, in a large measure, due to lack of good mental training. It is fairly obvious that everything which comes into the mind is *recorded* in consciousness, and this mental record is the basis of what we call 'memory'.

So the record which is the result of incoming psychic perceptions operates under the same mental laws as the mental record which is made by incoming physical sense perceptions.

**The Ability to Observe**

In the case of the psychometrist the incoming block of psychic impressions must be recorded and sent out again very quickly, in somewhat the same way as the visual impressions received by a television sports commentator must be put out again immediately as a running commentary on the game he is watching.

This means that the selective power of the mind must rapidly select incidents in the game in their correct sequence, and for the process to be carried out successfully, the first ability needed is the ability to *observe*. Observing in sequence is not quite so common as some people might imagine. Most of us, because of psychological blind spots, tend to observe some things and fail to observe others, or else we confuse the sequence in which things took place.

Trained observation is an essential for anyone using the psychic senses, and it is the lack of this which we referred to as a subsidiary cause of trouble in psychometric development. The fine psychic impulses which are received by the psychic must be realized, recorded and translated into vocal or written words, (some psychometrists do what is called 'postal psychometry'). If this is not done almost immediately, these impressions will merge into the general mental field, and become mixed with and distorted by the existing thought images therein.

An essential part of training, therefore, is the cultivation of this power of observation, and as we have said, this power is not quite so common, for, though all impressions are recorded in the mind, they rarely ever emerge into the waking consciousness, but remain below the mental threshold, in the subconsciousness. It is necessary, therefore, to train the mind to so operate that many more of these incoming impressions are recorded in the waking consciousness.

There are various exercises which have been devised to effect this training, but many of them suffer from being far too complex, in fact, that they defeat their own end. In all these matters the simpler an exercise can be made to be, the better its chance of success.

**Attention and Concentration**

Let us consider for a moment what 'observation' really is. It is the power to pay concentrated and consciously directed attention to the impressions which are aroused in our minds through the actions of our senses, as those senses react to all the various things and happenings which form the background of our lives.

This directed and concentrated attention means that it is necessary to develop the ability to keep the attention fixed on any part of that background at will. This, of course, is what is really meant by 'concentration'. So attention and concentration are both valuable training tools in psychometric development. Indeed, attention is also the key to much successful physical life also, and it should be noticed that the properly trained psychic, whether clairvoyant or psychometric, is not by any means the dreamy, impracticable person he is usually thought to be.

Of course, there are some psychics who *are* dreamy and impracticable, and there are several reasons for their being so. In the same way, there are many clergymen who to a greater or lesser extent present an image which closely resembles that which has been built up of them on the variety stage.

But just as we would not judge the great number of hardworking and efficient Christian priests and ministers by the vagaries of the few, so we should not judge the great number of psychics by the comparatively small number of impracticable 'freaks' to be found in the psychic field. In the cases of many of the freaks, this lack of mental training is one reason for their failure to help or impress the average man.

### False Spirituality

It must also be said that there is another and very strong influence at work which tends to encourage such people. This is the emotional and entirely uncritical approach to these matters by so many people. This usually stems from a curious superstition that these faculties are 'supernatural', and therefore their owners have a licence to be freakish. Also there is a continuing tradition that these same faculties are 'spiritual' gifts and many equate the idea of spirituality with vague sentiment, emotion and general 'out of this world' behaviour.

Because of this aura of false spirituality, their followers (for they usually get a 'following') will also equate the possession of psychic ability with spirituality. This leads to a form of hero-worship in which the unfortunate psychic is willy-nilly placed upon a pedestal, and in the eyes of his followers can do no wrong. When finally he does demonstrate that although psychic he is not spiritually developed, most of his followers will immediately kick away the pedestal and abandon him for another hero-figure. A minority of his followers will spend the rest of their lives in attempting to justify him at the bar of their own emotionally biased judgement.

## Incoming Psychic Impressions

It is for this reason that the genuine psychic needs a training which will enable him to be the master in his own mental sphere, and not dependent upon others. This is what the training in observation, attention and concentration gives to those who attempt it. It produces a mind which can register and sort out the incoming psychic impressions, which, as we have already pointed out, are very faint as compared with the impressions which are received through the *physical* senses.

Curiously enough, when once the psychometric faculty has been developed and trained, it is possible for these incoming impressions to equal and in some cases exceed the vividness of purely physical sensory perceptions.

## 'Conditioned Reflex'

The followers of certain 'occult' systems teach that the average person goes through life in a waking dream, responding automatically to conditions around him, and in general justifying the contention of the 'Behavourist' psychologists and the communistic Dialectical Materialists that a human being is but an elaborate piece of mechanism, working by what is termed 'conditioned reflex'.

The famous experiment of 'Pavlov's dogs' is regarded as proof of this mechanistic view of life, and these occult schools, though entirely disagreeing with the basic materialistic view, nevertheless say that the bulk of the thinking and action of the average man is the result of this 'conditioned reflex'. However, they definitely teach that it is possible for man to awaken from this dream and begin to act as a conscious being.

The further implications of this teaching would lead us too far from our chosen course, but we have mentioned it because it is an undoubted fact that to some extent or other, this dreamlike quality of consciousness does show itself in our waking life and work.

## Urban Life Blunts Perception

The conditions of modern life in urban surroundings tend to cause us to react *automatically* to conditions around us, whereas if we were living in wild natural surroundings, where inattention to the details of life would probably mean our death, we should find ourselves consciously observing everything near us in a way which we should never think of doing in urban life. Every sense impression which came into our mind would be consciously evaluated and as a result, the keenness of our physical sense would be greatly increased.

Even in modern urban life, it would greatly reduce the mortality rate due to 'accidents' if we learnt to pay attention to our surroundings, instead of walking or driving almost entirely automatically, depending merely upon the good sense of others, or the speed of our reflexes.

Now this does not mean that we should always be watching our environment with the same intensity as the white 'scout' used to have to employ in the days of the American Wild West, but it does mean that some part of that quality of intensity must be brought into ordinary life. This, in itself, would not be a bad thing.

**Kim's Game**

In some of my earlier writings, I mentioned a certain exercise in attention which is commonly known as 'Kim's Game', and which was taken from the book entitled *Kim* by Rudyard Kipling. Judging by comments from my readers, this exercise was found by many to be too difficult.

Much of this difficulty was, I think, psychological, for when one first starts this exercise, it is usually found to be somewhat disheartening. The reason for this is that it demonstrates very forcibly how poorly we are equipped with the mental power of attention. However, by steady application this particular exercise can develop the power in a reasonably short time.

For those who may not have heard of Kim's game, it is played by having a number of small objects, such as rings, coloured or carved buttons, small nuts, screws and other small engineering objects all placed upon a tray. For about two or three minutes one directs one's attention upon these things and then the tray is covered with a cloth. One now writes down the names of the objects which one remembers seeing on the tray. It is as well if one gets an acquaintance to collect together the various objects, but this is not really essential.

Having written down as many of the names of the objects as possible, the covering over the tray is removed, and a check made between the total number remembered and the actual number on the tray.

As a rough guide, if, out of twenty articles on the tray one can remember eight or nine, then the score is quite good. Mostly about five or six are the best that can be expected. With practice the power of recollection improves until a score of seventeen or eighteen out of twenty is possible.

When a reasonable score has been obtained, the exercise may be varied by attempting to recollect details of each object: its shape, the nature of any carving on it, its colour and any flaws which may have been noticed. Those who find that the element of competition helps them may try this exercise as a game, with one or two friends. Mostly, however, we are usually so ashamed of our initial failures that we prefer to play this game solo!

**Think Shoelace**

Here is another exercise, again, a simple one,

but very effective none the less. I call it 'Think Shoelace' since it was so described to me by my first teacher in these matters.

*Briefly it amounts to this, that the attention is fixed upon whatever one may be doing at the moment.* Thus, we are tying our shoelace. Then we simply put the whole of our attention on doing just that. We are not automatically tying the shoelace and at the same time listening, 'with half an ear' as we say, to the news on the radio, or the wife's voice as she gives us a list of what we must bring home when we return. Nor are we subjectively wondering what we ought to do at the office, or the works, in connection with some difficulties which may arise. No, we simply concentrate on tying that shoelace.

It sounds so simple that the idea of mental training resulting from it appears farcical, and we are liable to fall into the error of the gentleman in the Bible story who, on being told to wash in the waters of the Jordan to cure his leprosy, indignantly declared that the noted prophet who had given the advice should have done something spectacular: 'Stretched out his hand upon me' as he put it, and so made an instantaneous cure. In any case, they had some wonderful rivers, Abana and Pharpar, in his land. Real rivers, not like this little muddy and turbulent Jordan! However, as the story goes, the despised river cured the disease.

This curious desire for the bizarre and spectacular is one which has persisted through the ages, and we still find it in evidence today. It is this taste which causes many people to fall victims to the psychic and occult 'quacks' who are to be found in or around some of the societies and organizations devoted to the study of these matters.

The simplicity of this exercise is only apparent. When you have practised it a few times, you will have become aware of the tricks which your mind can play on you, given an opportunity.

The beauty of this simple exercise is that it can be practised at any time, without any involved preparation, and the least of its effects is an increased power of concentration, which alone can yield quite a reasonable dividend in daily life.

### The Faculty of Recollection

A further development is to extend this direct and conscious attention to whatever is happening around us as we catch the bus or train on our way to the factory or the office. How many of my readers, as they read these words, could remember the details of the house at the corner, as they turn from their own road into the main road? Its general appearance, how many windows, its decorations or its front garden (or lack of same)?

Again, the people in the bus or train, their appearance, their mannerisms, and so on. How many of us give them any but the slightest attention? Here are the materials for a rewarding mental exercise, and again, it is one which can be practised at any time.

Of course, such attention to other people does *not* mean that one needs to stare in a pop-eyed manner at them, which would be discourteous and might probably be productive of trouble, if they objected to being stared at. It is not necessary to stare fixedly for minutes at a time in order to retain a good visual picture of a person or object. This is an important point to remember. As a matter of fact, a quick glance, with concentrated attention, is sufficient.

In proof of this, let me give an account of visual recollection given me by a friend who is a hypnotist. He showed to someone a page of a book on psychology, having previously found out that the subject of psychology was one of which the person concerned knew nothing.

He then hypnotized her, and when she was in the deep hypnotic state he suggested to her that she was a popular lecturer and was standing on a platform ready to give a talk on the particular aspect of psychology which was touched upon in the page at which she had glanced for one minute only.

She immediately accepted the suggestion and gave quite a good lecturette upon what she had read in that brief glance at the page of the book on psychology. Where the page did not mention anything, then on that aspect she 'talked around' it, but where definite statements had been made, she elaborated on them and quoted word for word from the page itself.

This was after only one minute's glance at a page of small print. We have ourselves conducted similar experiments, with the same general results. Incidentally, it is this extremely powerful faculty of recollection possessed by the subconscious mind which so often falsifies what appear at first sight to be evidences of Extra-Sensory-Perception.

So it is not a question of the amount of time spent in observing anything or any person, but the intensity of attention which is required.

## Presentation of the Evidence

Here we come to a very important point in this training. You will remember that when we described the 'reading' given by a psychic we gave two versions of it, one by a psychometrist of the better kind, and the other by one whose work was greatly inferior. We said that it was in the *presentation* of the evidence that the difference between the two psychics was most apparent, and this links up with what we have just been saying about concentrated attention.

There is a 'technique of description', and this technique is not, as a general rule, learnt immediately. It involves a disciplined use of the attention, but once gained, it makes all the difference between success and failure. In our opinion, success in this descriptive technique is essential if you wish to carry out any work in this field. A similar technique is used by detectives, and also in the regulation work of the police.

Have you ever considered *how* you recognize a friend or acquaintance? Probably not, for most of us experience recognition in a subconscious manner, and can seldom say how we do it. It is necessary for us to examine this question fairly carefully.

There are, of course, certain things, certain salient points in connection with people, and in some cases such points are so strongly emphasized that recognition is often based entirely upon them. Thus, the nasal organ of Cyrano de Bergerac would identify him immediately, as would the crooked back of Richard III (if the Shakespearean image is correct). However, any or all of these most apparent points of recognition may be duplicated, and they are not so good for recognition purposes as some other aspects of the individual.

**The Finer Points of Identification**

One of these other points, and a very useful one, is the manner in which a person stands and moves. Each one of us has his own particular way of standing and moving around, and this comes to be associated with us in the minds of those whom we meet. In fact, there is what may be described as a whole group of such finer points, the nature of which definitely identifies us as a certain person.

Movements of the hands, the fingers and the feet, grimaces which become habitual to us, sudden turns of the head and changing tensions in the muscles of the face, especially around the eyes, all these, and many more, serve to identify us, and it is the identification afforded by these finer points which is very often the best evidence which can be given by the psychometrist.

### Description of Face and Form

After this, in order of importance comes the actual description of the face and form, the clothes and any points connected with them. Here again, the technique is a very definite one, and the general rule is that there should be coherence in the description given.

For instance, the budding psychometrist should not begin a description of the face he is perceiving psychically by stating that the man has blue eyes and a small wart on his neck. He should start first of all by describing any *outstanding feature* on the face, such as the large nose of which we have spoken, or the absence of part of one ear, or the absence of one eye.

Then he should proceed to describe the face, starting with the colour and texture of the hair, whether it is smoothly dressed or sticks up in an unruly fashion. Then the forehead, whether it is broad and high or low and narrow, lined with wrinkles or smooth.

The eyebrows thick or thin, bushy or smooth; the eyes, their colour, their setting in the face, close together or far apart, lines and sagging muscles around them, deeply set or somewhat protruding; the nose, aquiline, straight or *retroussè*, broad or thin around the nostrils; the ears, large or small, how set on the head; the cheeks, full and round or sunken, florid or pale, general complexion; moustache and/or beard, type, shape and general colour and appearance; mouth and lips, full lips or thin lips; jaw and chin, firm or otherwise, general type of face, round, square or lantern-jawed; neck, thin or thick, long or short.

**Automatic Sequence of Attention**

All this would seem at first sight to be a very formidable task, but as we *always* register these and other details every time we look at a person (though the bulk of the detail remains below the threshold of consciousness) it is not the mere registration of the details which calls for some training on the part of the beginner.

What *is* important is the gradual building-up of an *automatic sequence of attention*, so that all the details are stored in their correct pigeon-holes in the subconscious, from which they can be drawn in the same sequence.

This technique also applies to the details of the body, the arms and legs, the dress and all connected with it. Obviously, there are certain general characteristics which should be described at the very beginning of the description. The height, general type of body (fat or thin) and any outstanding details such as an artificial leg, are some of these.

Then we come to the more subtle points of stance, etc., which we have already spoken of, and it is here that often the most convincing bits of evidence may be gained. To summarize what we have been saying on this question of accurate description, we would suggest the following general sequence:

1. Estimated height and build of person perceived, together with any outstanding peculiarities, such as an artificial leg or deformity of any kind.
2. Clothing, style and colour.
3. Quick detailed description of features, any peculiarities to be noted and described first.
4. Any finer points of identification, mannerisms, and so on.

**Personal Talents**

What we have just given applies to the descriptions of people, but, of course, the same principles apply in the case of landscapes and such general surroundings as may be given. Now that you have the principle involved, you may apply it in your own way. Indeed, in all psychic work, there is an area where the *personal* talents come into play, just as they do in painting and sculpture, for instance.

You will remember that we have said that all psychic work is as much an art as a science. Here is where your own individual talent may be employed, and it is here that new discoveries may be made.

So don't be afraid to experiment in this field. The outline given is a general one, and as long as you have the principle of *sequential description* fixed in your mind, you may vary the application in accordance with your own particular 'slant'.

Remember that even with such sequential description, it is possible for you to get into a rigid groove, and this may prevent further progress in your work. It was Oliver Wendell Holmes, in one of his books, who said; 'the difference between a grave and a groove is only one of depth'.

So preserve flexibility of mind. Use the techniques both psychological and psychic which you have been given here until you are perfectly familiar with them, and can rely upon them. Then, as your knowledge and experience grow, you can adapt them to your own individual method of working.

Remember always that your subconsciousness has its own point of view, which does not always agree with that of the waking self, and unless you give this hidden aspect of yourself a chance to express itself, it may begin to work against your efforts. We shall return to this later on.

**Control of Emotional Reactions**

Here we come to another very important factor, namely, the place of emotion in our psychometric work. Very often, as we attempt to psychometrize an article, we find the emotional atmosphere which we are sensing is beginning to flood our mind, and we feel very acutely the sorrow or pain or anger connected with the object.

Now this empathy, or 'feeling-with', is of the very essence of psychometric work, but if we allow it to dominate our consciousness, then we lose control of our emotional reactions and so obliterate the fine psychic impressions which are coming in.

A perfect analogy is to be found in the well-known radio phenomenon of 'oscillation'. A radio set may, under certain conditions, not only receive the signals on a particular wave-length, but may also re-radiate them in a distorted form as the piercing whistle or howl with which we are all familiar. In the early days of radio this phenomenon was very common, but the tuning devices which have since been developed have largely eliminated it, though, under certain conditions it can still occur.

**Controlling Emotional Reactions**

In the same way, it is possible to sense the

emotional record of the object you are handling and be so affected by it as to lose all contact with the psychic impressions and simply flounder in a sea of emotion, without realizing that the whole thing is out of focus, and what may be a mild emotional record has been enormously exaggerated by your own reactions.

It is well, therefore, if you can train yourself to control your emotional reactions, and one of the best exercises for this is a very old one indeed. It is a simple one, too, and consists in making yourself listen to some highly emotional attack upon one of your own pet subjects.

If you are a Conservative in politics, then listen to a violent communist attack upon your political creed; if you are a Socialist, then listen to a die-hard Conservative attacking all the ideas which seem to you to be so important. The same technique can be used on religious, artistic or sociological ideas.

The important thing is that you must *not* sit and listen in a state of suppressed wrath, but neither must you impose upon yourself a mental state of passive resistance. You must simply listen *calmly and attentively* to the statements made, assenting or disagreeing with them *mentally, not emotionally*.

Remember that the ideas which seem so repulsive to you are tidings of joy to the one to whom you are listening, and in the same way the ideas which to you seem so self-evidently true are equally repulsive to him.

A few experiments along these lines will soon convince you of the part emotion plays in what we are usually pleased to term 'rational thought'.

Even in the realm of mathematics, which at one time was thought to be practically the only non-emotional subject, we can find the same emotional bias at work as the different propounders of new systems of geometry and the revolutionary hypothesis of Relativity get into print or fulminate against each other at the meetings of learned societies.

**Is Training Necessary?**

Many people develop the faculty of psychometry without any such mental training as that which we have outlined in this chapter, and some may ask whether all this 'training' is necessary. The short answer is that it is not absolutely necessary, but it can be of tremendous help.

In the same way, there are those who are born with an innate sense of music and rhythm, and who can perform on a musical instrument in quite a creditable fashion. Others are born musical prodigies, but the work of both types is tremendously increased if they learn the theory and technique of music.

So there are many who have gained the faculty of psychometry without any training, except perhaps that given in a 'development circle' and they can carry out quite good work. However, it so often happens that the faculty has been misdirected and employed for purposes which to many of us would appear to be outside the legitimate scope of psychometry.

This is particularly the case where psychometry is used in an attempt to contact discarnate people. That this attempt may sometimes be successful, as many years of experience in these fields gives us reason for believing, does not mean that this is always the case, and we deplore the use of the faculty in this way.

We are of the opinion that there are other and better ways of effecting such contact, and we would strongly suggest that it is most desirable that this wonderful faculty be taken out of the sectarian religious atmosphere in which it is usually to be found, and treated in an objective fashion. Equally, and with even more urgency, we would try to rescue it from the base uses made of it by the professional fortune-telling element which infests the fringe of the psychic movement.

# CHAPTER FOUR

# FIRST STEPS

Human nature being what it is, we expect that quite a number of our readers will have turned to this chapter without reading anything that has gone before, which is a pity, but it is not uncommon. However, it gives us the chance to point out that although it is really better to undertake the preliminary training, before attempting to do practical work, much of that training can be carried out together with the actual psychometrical work. At the same time, it does impose an extra strain upon the developing psychic, and we would suggest that, having browsed through this chapter, our would-be psychometrists go back to the work outlined in the previous chapter, and begin on that, making occasional experiments in the actual 'sensing' technique.

## Psychometrical Sensings

Such an approach will, as we have said, yield dividends, for the more the mind has been brought under some kind of discipline, the more reliable the psychometrical sensings will be.

It will be noted that we speak of *sensing*', and this is the best way of describing what happens when one attempts to psychometrize an article. Such sensing is a general impression which is received, and for quite a time, unless the experimenter has the visual or aural forms of perception strongly developed, it will remain simply an impression.

Then, as development proceeds, the visual and/or audible images will begin to show themselves. Remember, *all* perception, whether physical or super-physical, is, in fact a development of *one* basic set of impressions.

On the physical plane, the sense of 'touch' is the basic sense, and each of the five senses is a different kind of 'touching'. Thus, the rays of light touch the sensitive retina of our eye, and cause certain chemical and electrical changes there and in the optic nerves. These changes are transmitted to the sight-centre in the brain, and are there, in some mysterious manner, translated into visual impressions.

Sound waves striking the ear drum cause movement in the complicated 'hammer-and-stirrup bones' of the mechanism of the ear, and this movement affects the fluid in a special canal which also contains many nerve fibres. From these fibres chemical and electrical changes are transmitted to the centre in the brain which governs hearing, and are there translated into audible impressions.

In just the same way the senses of taste, and smell operate; all five senses being based upon the one sense of touch, which was the first sense to emerge in evolutionary time.

## A Single Immediate Perception

In exactly the same way, though after another mode, the psychic perceptions work. Actually, the psychic is a single immediate perception, conveying direct knowledge to the self, but as the mind has developed in a certain way, through the specialization of the physical senses, the psychic impressions which are received are, as a general rule translated automatically into the physical sense images with which we are familiar.

So in the first stages of development, it is this general impression which will be received and you must not be disappointed if for a long time you get such impressions without any visual or audible images.

At a much later stage in your development, if you have persevered so far, there will come a time when the pictures and auditory images will give place to a formless perception which, however, will give you all and more than you ever received through the images. At the same time, you will retain the power to use the picture – impressions if you so wish.

## Later Development

However, this later stage of development will not as a general rule come for some considerable time after you have started your development, and, indeed, it need not ever appear unless you yourself aspire to its unfoldment.

For some of you, such further development

would possibly be out of your reach, and you would be well advised to stick to and train the 'form' type of psychometry.

Now although we have said that the impressions give way to the images of various kinds, nevertheless there is always a background of impressional sensing which accompanies the pictures seen or the sounds heard, and this background is important in enabling you to interpret that which you perceive. We will return to this question of impressional atmosphere later.

**Preparing for a Reading**

Now you are ready to commence your actual psychometrical development. What are the main points to be observed? The first, we think, is that for successful work you should be as comfortable as possible. No tight clothing, ill fitting shoes which give pain, no uncomfortable seat; though it is as well if you avoid the other extreme in the matter of seating, for you can be *too* comfortable.

As far as possible, you should be relaxed physically. A good way to achieve this is to use a combined breathing-and-relaxation exercise such as the following.

Sit comfortably, but do not cross the legs; keep the feet firmly on the floor, and take care that the edge of the chair you are sitting on does not catch you just behind the knees and so impede the circulation in your legs. Let your hands rest on your knees. Now take in a deep breath, and breathe out slowly, at the same time quietly fixing your mental attention upon the top of the head, and as you continue to exhale, allow that attention to travel down over all your body, until at the end of the breathing-out it has reached your feet. Now take in another breath and repeat the process.

The essence of the exercise is that as you allow your attention to sweep down over the body, so, at every point reached you *must also relax the muscles of that part.* You will find that at first you will not be able to keep all the muscles relaxed; some of them, particularly the muscles of the face and neck will more or less automatically tense up again as soon as your attention has passed on to the next part of your body. Do not worry about this, just proceed with the exercise. In time the muscles will remain relaxed after the attention has passed them.

At first half a dozen inbreathings and outbreathings will be enough, but this is something which you will have to judge for yourself. The success of the exercise is seen when you find that the body as a whole appears to be considerably relaxed.

## Choosing the Objects

You are now ready to attempt your first reading. Which brings us to the question of what objects you should choose for your first experiments, for objects vary greatly in the record which can be obtained from them, and in your early days it is as well if you choose those which give the strongest and most easily read impressions.

Before discussing the kinds of objects, it may be as well to consider where they may be obtained. If you can enlist the aid of one or two friends, who can supply them, and who can check up on the accuracy of your 'reading', you will have a considerable advantage, since you will not have to demonstrate your faculty to people who may be sceptical or even antagonistic to the subject.

It is as well, also, if you do not know very much of your friends' private lives, since such prior knowledge may quite easily confuse you and in any case will detract from the value of whatever you may read from the object.

**Two 'Memories'**

There are two main 'memories' connected with every object. The first is what we may call the inherent or personal memory of the object's individual and separate existence. Then there is what we may term the 'gathered' memory. This is the sum of all the impressions which have been made upon it by its association with human beings, and this will give highly complex memories which need considerable skill to read.

Of course, it usually happens that one stratum or another in this composite memory is so powerful that it dominates the rest, and prevents you from going more deeply into the general memory connected with its history. It is suggested, therefore, that in your initial experiments you select objects which have either a powerful primary or inherent memory-aura, or which have not passed through many hands.

It is best, of course, if the object has been connected with one person only, as it is then unnecessary for you to have to try to sort out the memory layers connected with the various people to whom the object may have belonged. The simpler your initial experiments can be made, the better. Later, as you gain confidence in your powers, you can attempt to psychometrize more difficult objects..

Necklaces usually make good articles for reading, but rings and very small objects are more difficult. Keys are not good objects, for they are apt to pass through several hands; neither are handkerchiefs or other washable articles, for the repeated processes of washing and being handled by others make it difficult to pick up the aura-memory.

If you attempt to psychometrize gloves, it is best to turn them inside out, as the outer surfaces will have collected extraneous impressions.

Letters are a good source, but if you do experiment with them remember that the envelope has passed through several hands, and is of very little use. You should therefore remove the letter from its envelope before attempting to psychometrize it. Perhaps we may start our description of your first attempts in psychometry by taking the letter as the object used.

### Technique of Sensing

You can spread the letter on the table and rest the palm of your hand on it. Or you may just put your fingertips on the signature, or hold the letter to your forehead. It is for you to find for yourself the method which best suits *you*; every person has his own peculiarity in this matter.

Preferably, as we have indicated, the writer of the letter should not be known to you personally, though, of course, it should be possible to obtain some knowledge about him after your reading, as otherwise it will be impossible for you to verify the truth or falsity.

Having taken up the letter, you will now make a simple act of will or 'intention' to the effect that you are going to read the psychic record of this letter. Just a simple intention is all that is necessary; a sufficient indication to your subconsciousness that you wish any incoming impressions which may be picked up to be passed through to your waking self. This is a 'trigger action' concerning which we shall say something later.

You now quietly wait until you become conscious of new and different impressions coming into your mind. These impressions may remain as simple impressions, or they may be accompanied by vivid pictures and inner sounds. Sometimes the pictures will arise without any surrounding impressions, but whatever you get should be described to the friend who is assisting you in your experiments by acting as an auditor. Should you be compelled to work without such help, then a good tape-recorder can be used to record your description.

**Bodily Sensations**

You will often feel yourself impelled to react strongly to the impressions you are getting, but if you are wise you will not allow this reaction to flood your field of consciousness and arouse similar conditions in your own self. You may also, and this is a frequent happening in psychometry, receive bodily sensations, indications of illness or accident, and these impressions may be very strong indeed. Never allow them to influence you in any undesirable fashion.

Remember that you are open to all the influences coming from the object you are 'reading', and that means that you often sense conditions which you do not like, just as you also sense conditions which appeal to you. You must not, however, be selective at this stage in your development, but must allow all the impressions which are being received to come up into consciousness.

At a later date you *can* be selective, and follow one particular train of psychic images, but at first this is not possible. At the same time you must not allow any undesirable impression to affect you too strongly. When this seems likely to happen, it is best to put down the object and break your contact with it. This is sometimes done by the psychometrist washing his hands before starting to contact another article, but it can also be done by a simple act of will, a definite intention to break the contact.

### Necessity for Discrimination

What you often get, and this applies particularly to letters, is an impression of the personality of the owner or writer, and this can be both evidential and useful. Remember, however, if the writer of the letter or the owner of the object has recently suffered a great shock, or has been under considerable mental and emotional strain, then you will, in all probability pick up this condition before anything else.

So even in the simplest reading, you will find that it is necessary to use a good deal of discrimination, and not to accept all your impressions at their face value. Thought has a very real existence, apart from the mind and emotions which formulated it, and the results of such thinking are often most strongly impressed upon the object, and may well be read off by you as impressions of actual occurrences. In the same way, clairvoyants often find it extremely difficult to differentiate between such emotionally charged thought images and actual astral beings or conditions.

**A Curious Intuition**

This discrimination will develop as you continue to practice psychometry. You will find that you are developing a curious intuition which enables you to perceive the subtle differences between the impressions due to thought and those due to actual physical activity. This subtle perception is something well worth cultivating, as its use can be extended to many other fields of experience.

When describing the impressions you are receiving you should always aim at presenting as balanced a picture as possible. If you must err, then it is best to err on the side of brevity rather than on the side of long-windedness.

Although the psychic impressions are received in the subconsciousness in a block, you will find that in practice they emerge into the waking consciousness at varying speeds. In some cases you may have to wait for quite a long time before any impression comes through, and such a slow rate of emergency may continue.

With other objects you will find that the impressions come pouring through at a very rapid rate. So don't be worried if the impressions seem to 'dribble' into your mind, or if, on the other hand they are so rapid that it seems impossible to make a note of them.

Again, the strength of the personality of the owner of the object will very often force these impressions upon it in such a way that they form the strongest layer of influence connected with it, and they will therefore be the first to be sensed by you.

**Increase of Accuracy**

It very often happens that the particular health conditions of the owner of the article may be sensed by you and in some cases this sensing may be so strong that you actually feel the pains that are felt by him to such an extent they seem to be actually in your own body.

This could be undesirable, unless you deliberately and with intention break the contact with the object you are psychometrizing. In a later section we will suggest to you a method which will enable you to break any particular contact and also to 'tune in', as it were, to any aspect of the general block of psychic impressions received from any object. This, however, is best done after you have begun to get some actual results from your experiments.

At first you may find that out of ten statements you may make about any object, perhaps two will be more or less accurate, one may bear relation to the actual state of things, and the rest may be either somewhat near or else far from the mark.

With practice, this proportion will gradually change, and as you gain confidence the proportion of 'hits' to 'misses' may be sixteen or seventeen out of twenty.

When you have arrived at this stage, then you may consider yourself to be quite a good psychometrist.

Above all things, 'to thine own self be true', for it is no part of our work along these lines to encourage you to lower your standards of truth, nor do we desire to hoodwink you into any self-deception.

## Record of Experimental Work

Keep a record of your experimental work, and record not only the successes but also the failures. Never be afraid to admit that you *have* failures, but use the failures as means whereby you can discover the laws underlying your work.

There are psychic tides and currents which will work for you or against you, there are psychic tides within your own inner self which may work with or against the outer tides and influences, and there is also that imponderable factor: the influence of your own personality upon your psychometry. As we have already said, this partakes of the nature of science *and* art.

Learn to observe your own reactions to the impressions you receive. You will find that to some of them you give a welcome, to others you erect a barrier. Try to find out why this is; endeavour to understand your personal equation, and above all things, never consciously twist or alter what you receive either to impress others or to excuse yourself.

## Conditions of Illness or Death

Now we wish to touch upon another point. This is, how you should present your 'reading'. It sometimes happens that conditions of illness or even death are strongly felt, and here you must be extremely careful not to express this impression in a way which might cause the person concerned to auto-suggest themselves into the idea that the condition is one that cannot be altered or that death is inevitable.

We have heard some very reprehensible statements made in this way by psychometrists and we would most strongly urge upon you that you give out these impressions in such as way as to give warning of difficulties ahead, together with whatever impressions you may have as to how these difficulties may be surmounted.

Remember this: even when you have attained quite a considerable proficiency in this work, you are still far from being able to act as Sir Oracle. In the first stages you most certainly are not in any such position of infallibility.

We are strongly moved to emphasize this point because we have seen how harmful such statements can be. Friends of ours were told such things and the results in their lives were disastrous. For this reason we would urge you to exercise discretion in these things.

## Importance of Discretion

Here we touch upon another thing. We have just used the word 'discretion'. Many psychics have a nasty habit of discussing with others the information they have received psychically about other people. This is inexcusable on any count.

The attitude of the psychometrist should be that of the doctor or lawyer; whatever he learns through the exercise of his psychic faculty should be regarded as entirely confidential and should not be divulged to any other person.

We have seen so much trouble arise through a failure to observe this rule, that we would impress it upon you with all the force in our power. Such malicious or ignorant gossip is one of the reasons why so many cultured and intelligent people are turned away from the whole subject, and these are just the people whom we would wish to become interested.

## Selective Working

When you have begun to gain some proficiency in psychometrizing objects in the way we have described, then you should begin to employ what we may term a 'selective' method of working. So far, you have been passively receiving whatever impressions and pictures entered your mind as you 'read' the object. Now you must learn to develop the power to direct your psychic vision in any way you wish.

You must actively reach out for the information you desire, instead of passively receiving whatever may come along. Such a power of selection, once acquired, is a distinct step forward in your development and gives you an increasing control over your own faculty.

There are two ways in which this may be done. In the first way a general intention is made by asking a definite question and this question must be put in simple and pictorial terms. The more pictorial it is, the better chance it has of being answered by the psychic faculty of the person concerned.

An actual example may help to illustrate this point. If we wish to obtain information along one particular line connected with the object being psychometrized, we take the article and make the usual passive contact with it. As a general rule, there then builds up in our mind a whirling sphere of greyish mist, in which small starry points of light gleam. Each point of light is the starting place of a line of knowledge concerning the object and those linked with it.

We now mentally ask the question we have in mind, and at once one of the points of light appears to *become significant*, and as we look at it, a stream of impressions referring to the question asked begins to pour into our mind. This is one method in which a positive action is brought into play.

**The Tree of Life**

The second way in which selective contact may be made is by using a 'Key Symbol'. This symbol has been linked with a particular emotional and mental idea. Thus, a key-symbol which could be used could be an orange coloured circle with the symbol of the planet Mercury in its centre. This particular symbol is one of a set of ten which together form what is called 'The Tree of Life', and this is one of the very important group of symbols used in a certain occult philosophy known as the Qabalah. For further information on this great group-symbol, our book entitled *Magic and the Qabalah*, published by the Aquarian Press may be consulted.

The symbol of Mercury has special reference to all matters concerning mentality: books, lecturing, conveying information by any means (Mercury or Hermes, as the Greeks called him; was the Messenger of the Gods) such as letters, cables, telegrams or personal conversation. So if it is desired to obtain by psychometrical means some information as to the intellectual calibre of the writer of a letter which is being psychometrized, then this symbol would serve as an excellent key-symbol, and keep the psychic impressions routed along the one line, to the exclusion of irrelevant matters.

*But the key symbol must have been thought out and linked in the mind with the characteristic to which it was to be the key.* So you would have to make your own key-symbols, though, of course you could use the symbol system of the Tree of Life as your basis.

**Colour Symbolism**

There is also the question of colour symbolism. You will find that you will receive many impressions of colour in connection with objects you psychometrize, and in some cases the colour will appear quite vividly before you. There is a general code of colour symbols, and this may be found in such a book as *Man, Visible and Invisible*, by Annie Besant and C.W. Leadbeater.

However, you will also discover that your inner self has its own particular meanings which it attaches to various colours, and *for you* this is much better than simply relying upon the findings of others. So you will have to work out your own scale of colour symbolism, and this in itself will be of considerable value to you in your development, as you will discover.

Incidentally, some psychometrists regard strong vibrant colours as relatively 'low' and 'earthly', and delicate pastel shades as being 'high' and 'spiritual'. Do not fall into this particular trap. The strong vibrant colours are just as 'high' as the weak pastel shades. In these matters, you must use your own reason and not slavishly follow others.

**Flower Psychometry**

There is a curious form of 'sensing' which is very often demonstrated in public meetings for psychometry. It is usually called 'Flower Psychometry' and the procedure is as follows. The querent brings a flower to the meeting, and this flower is psychometrized in the usual way. Before coming to the meeting, the person concerned takes the flower he has picked (which is the best procedure) or bought (which it not such a good procedure) and holding the flower he considers in his mind any particular problem which is worrying him, and upon which he desires advice.

In a great many cases it is this problem which is picked up by the psychometrist, and the resulting advice may come from his own mental point of view, or be derived from the psychic impressions which he receives from the flower. In any case, the flower has provided a link between the querent and the psychometrist.

**Flower Aura**

The explanation which is given of this particular method is that around every object there is a psychic atmosphere or 'aura' as it is called. In objects generally this aura, which carries the records, is complex, as it has been subjected to so many influences at various times in its history, and for this reason it is more difficult for the psychometrist to pick up any particular past.

But the aura of the flower, which is also a *living* thing, is much more of a blank sheet, a *tabula rosa* and the strong thought and emotion impressed on it by the querent will be far more easily picked up.

The budding psychic may try experiments with floral psychometry, but we would strongly impress upon him that he should continue to experiment with all kinds of objects, bearing complex psychic records, and not remain content with this elementary method.

It is very easy to fall into this trap, but if you do, then you will have limited your psychometric powers considerably, since the use of the triggering key-symbols is just as effective as the floral contact, and can yield much more information.

**Experiments for Greater Proficiency**

The main thing to remember is that you should never be content to stay at one level. Always you should be pressing forward to greater proficiency, and you should never be afraid to make experiments. Those which you can think up for yourself will usually prove more fruitful than those suggested to you by others, as they will usually be the results of some effective thinking which has taken place in your deeper mind.

At the same time you should be on the look-out for new suggestions for further experiments. Let us give you an illustration of what we mean. A number of years ago, we attended a public demonstration of psychometry given by a certain Captain Bland. During this demonstration he showed us an interesting experiment.

Instead of holding an object in his hand in order to psychometrize it, Captain Bland asked the owner of it to place it on a table some ten feet away from him. He then concentrated his attention upon it for a moment and proceeded to give a very evidential reading concerning it.

Here an interesting point was raised, for there are those who say that the psychometrist reads the record which is held in the 'aura' of the article, in a similar fashion to the dog which follows a man by the actual scent he leaves upon the ground and upon everything he touches, whilst others maintain that the object, being by its actual existence linked with all its associated records in the Universal Mind and the mind of the psychometrist, through the images it calls up in his mind.

The foregoing sounds somewhat involved, though if one substitutes the term 'Akashic Record' for 'Universal Mind', it is the theory held very largely in the East. The other concept, which we call the 'Bloodhound theory' is, perhaps more easily accepted by the average person than the metaphysical oriental idea. May we suggest that both views are correct, but each needs the other to round it out fully.

At one time we did a good deal of

experimentation along this line, and the idea which we have tentatively put forward is really based upon our findings in these experiments.

**Charged Objects**

Now we come to a more recondite aspect of our subject. When we gave an imaginative description of the average psychometry reading, we included in it a ring which had once been in ecclesiastical hands, and we did this for a definite reason.

In an earlier part of this book we referred to three kinds of impressions which it was possible to receive, but later we referred to only two of these. One was the record of the article itself, its basic nature and manufacture. Then came the gathered memories which it had acquired in its use by human beings under differing circumstances.

There is, however, another set of impressions which an object may carry, and these are impressions that have been deliberately imposed upon the object by the will of some being, whether such a being was human, sub-human or super-human.

Very often the impressions which have been made upon the object partake of the qualities of all three grades of intelligence. Here, of course, we are to some extent touching upon some aspects of being which are regarded by many 'moderns' as being entirely fictional.

Angels and fairies are relegated to the

phantasies of childhood, and learned anthropoligists spin wonderful theories to explain the records in every part of the world which appear to indicate that forms of life other than those using material bodies have been seen by many people under many different conditions.

However, because of our own personal experience in this field, we feel pretty sure that there are good reasons for the continuing belief in the existence of such intelligences.

**Borders of the Magical**

Here, we are stepping upon the borders of the magical. Anyway, we are going to place before you certain ideas and suggest certain experiments which may be of interest to those of you who wish to go beyond the mere giving of psychometrical 'readings'.

Perhaps this is the point where we should give the details of an important aspect of your development. If you were concerned with certain chemical work, you would have learnt a little trick which often saves the chemist quite a lot of trouble. He may want to know what is in a given bottle or flask, from which the label had been removed, and, of course, if identification by sight is not possible, the natural procedure is to open the bottle and see what it smells like inside.

Here there is a possibility of danger, for the substance may be highly toxic and highly volatile, so that before you can get it out of your lungs you may have been affected by it. The trick is first to take a good deep breath and then, holding that breath in the lungs, take a further sniff at the contents of the bottle.

Your lungs, being filled with air do not take in any quantity of the gas which is given off by whatever substance is being tested, but sufficient reaches the olfactory nerves for you to identify it. If it is something very irritating or dangerous, the lungs can immediately be emptied, and the released air sweeps out with it the very small trace of the lethal element which may be in the nose. In the past we have found this little trick has saved us quite a lot of trouble.

**Receptive Attitude**

We have mentioned it here because your approach to what we propose to call 'charged objects' should resemble such a method of dealing with whatever force you may contact in connection with such articles, of which, for instance, the ring which we mentioned in our 'psychometric reading' is one.

It is necessary that you approach such objects with the correct attitude of mind. This should be a positive intention to read the record of the object. Then, following this triggering-off action, the mind should be kept receptive, but still positive.

This attitude has been described by a Roman Catholic writer, the late Monsignor R.H. Benson as comparable to the flight of a seagull hovering practically motionless against a strong gale. We know that in spite of its apparent immobility, the gull is working very hard indeed to stay in the one place.

So the receptive attitude of which we have spoken should also be the 'receptive point' of a strong mental intention. This attitude of mind is not acquired at the first attempt, and it is for this reason that we have reserved our treatment of these charged objects until we have given you the more simple and easily acquired techniques.

**Misuse of 'Mystical'**

Incidentally, in case any of our readers are led by our reference to R.H. Benson to think that he became a convert to psychic teachings, we may say that the illustration was used by him in connection with a book of stories on mysticism, and this has very little to do with psychic phenomena.

It is true that certain psychic phenomena very often appear in the lives of the mystics, but they are regarded as hindrances, not helps to the mystical life. This, by the way, is true also of Buddhism and some other Oriental religions. They all strongly oppose the development of the psychic powers, which, they say, are like toys which lure a person away from the spiritual path, and at best are time-wasters.

The word 'mystical' is greatly misused in these modern times, and made to refer to psychic and occult phenomena. At some date in the future we hope to be able to discuss the relative values, *as we see them*, of psychism, occultism and mysticism, in another book.

**Talismans and Charms**

Examples of 'charged objects' are talismans and charms, the virtues of which are extolled in the various psychic and occult publications. Some of these are sold on the well-known dictum of the American showman, Barnum, 'There's one born every minute', but others have been carefully made by people who have a good working knowledge of the principles of magic.

The first class of charged objects works primarily by auto-suggestion on the part of their possessors, but the second class really has power apart from such auto-suggestion, and it is the objects in this second class which should be approached with caution.

If it is known that one has, or is developing, psychic powers, the offering of such an object for a 'reading' is common practice, and it is as well to take due precautions. After all, you have not attempted to develop psychometric powers in order to be 'butchered to provide a psychic holiday', if we may somewhat transpose a saying regarding the ancient Roman gladiators.

We come now to the second class of 'charged objects' and these are those which have been blessed or consecrated by the priests of some Christian and non-Christian bodies. Of such was the ring which our hypothetical querent put up for a psychometric reading. Here the influence radiating from the object is keyed (if the blessing or consecration has been properly carried out, and not in the perfunctory manner characteristic of some ecclesiastics) to a high moral and ethical level, and the effect of it cannot but be helpful.

Even here, however, it is advisable to approach such an object with the same mental attitude as that used in the case of the other type of subject.

**An Exercise in Charging Objects**

Now we may suggest that you carry out certain experiments of your own in connection with these 'charged objects'. This will require the co-operation of a sympathetic friend, and if this friend has a good power of visualization, so much the better.

The exercise is carried out in the following way: five pieces of wood, say about three inches long and an inch wide (thickness immaterial) are taken and marked either by numbers or letters, so that they can be distinguished from each other. The one who is to 'charge' them then enters in a notebook exactly what strong emotion he wishes to impress upon each one. As this is best done by visual images, he should also enter in the notebook the images he proposes to use in each case.

We will suppose that the object marked 'A' is to be charged with the emotion of anger. He may use any image which he thinks gives a good picture of this emotion, and, holding the object between his hands, he builds up the picture as strongly as possible, at the same time endeavouring to feel the emotion which it portrays.

Having done this, he wraps the object in a piece of silk and turns his attention to the next object. It is advisable, by the way, to allow a period of some fifteen minutes or so for him to clear the emotional bias from his mind, otherwise the influences on the next object will be somewhat mixed.

This work should be carried on until all five objects have been charged. Of course, during this work you should not have been in the same room, neither should you have been within earshot of what was going on. For preference it would be best for you to be out of the house altogether.

### 'Reading' the Objects

Now the objects are handed to you, or you take them up one by one yourself, unwrap them only as you do so, and then give your 'reading', endeavouring to describe the general emotional effect, together with any pictures which may come up.

Having dealt with the first article, you pass on to the second, unwrap it and repeat the process, and so on with them all. It is as well if, after each reading, you rub your hands vigorously together as though rubbing off dust. Some psychometrists wash their hands after each reading, but this is really unnecessary, and, indeed, is impossible if you are giving a public demonstration.

The readings which were given for each object are now compared with the entry made in the notebook by the one who 'charged' them, and successes and failures noted down.

This is a very good exercise, for when you do begin to be able to sense these different emotions in this way, you are increasing your ability to select just that particular line which you wish to follow through, from out of the mass of information which you receive from any article.

Once you are able to pick up these influences in this way, you can use the faculty to sense the conditions of any room or house you may enter, and this may be helpful to you at a later date.

**Person-Psychometry**

Finally, it is also possible for you to psychometrize a *person*, by directing your intention towards him and then picking up the images and sensings which come into consciousness. Here is a big field for experimentation.

Incidentally, you will find in connection with this 'person-psychometry' that most people carry around in their aura quite a few definite thought-forms, and in some cases these forms have considerable emotional energy locked up in them. Some may be the result of intensive visualization; they may have been reading a gripping and exciting novel, and the characters in the story have been so clearly visualized that they exist in the aura as well-defined forms which may easily be picked up by the psychometrist.

Another interesting phenomenon may also be experienced in this psychometrizing of persons. Apart from imaginary characters from novels one sometimes sees other forms, which when described by us are usually not recognized by the person concerned. If, however, the form is sufficiently striking in appearance, the person may say, 'that's nothing to do with me, but it *is* a very good description of a man who called on us this week, and caused a bit of a row!'

The key is in the latter part of that remark. The strong emotional reactions aroused have caused the image of the one concerned to be strongly imprinted on the aura, and so be easily seen and described by the psychometrist. We have, on occasion, amused ourselves by describing such 'imprints', as we call them, to someone whom we had just met, and concerning whom we knew nothing at all. The results were often striking.

In a later piece of writing dealing with the subject of 'reading the aura', we hope to go more fully into this and other aspects of what we have called 'personality-psychometry'.

## Diagnostic Psychometry

There is another interesting application of psychometry. This is what we may call 'diagnostic psychometry'. It is an occult teaching that disease in the physical body originates in the subtle 'etheric double' which is the background to the physical body, and upon which the physical body is continually being built up and broken down, so that we do not possess the same material body that we had say five years ago. (Some medical authorities say two years see a complete exchange of physical matter in the body.)

So, according to this occult teaching, the etheric body is the *real* persisting body, which we keep during our entire life, and it is in this body that the first symptoms of disease are to be found, long before any purely physical symptoms are felt or signs seen which can provide material for diagnosis by the doctor.

It is during this 'pre-matter' phase that disease may best be dealt with by the more subtle methods of homoeopathic medicine and so-called 'spiritual healing', though, of course, these methods can be quite successfully applied even when the disease has gained a strong hold on the actual material body.

## Physical Contact Unnecessary

In this field of psychometry great care is required, for there are many people who can be adversely affected by such a diagnosis because of auto-suggestion on their part, and this can and has led to tragedies in the past.

If you should decide to follow up this line of work, it would help you greatly if you followed the example of a friend of mine who took a two-year course in anatomy and physiology before commencing.

In the first stages of the development of this phase of psychometry you should move your hand over the subject's body, keeping at least three inches away from actual physical contact with the person. It is *never necessary* in this diagnostic work to make any physical contact with the body of the person concerned. If you break this rule, then you align yourself with those malpractitioners whose aims are sexual, not psychic, and you will build up untold trouble for yourself on all levels.

For the same reason, if you ever do this kind of work, *always* have a third person present during any interview. We have referred to this form of psychometry, since it is a very interesting phase of the work, but personally speaking, we would not advise you to take it up on any large scale.

Another interesting phase of the work is that of distinguishing 'fake' jewels from the real variety, fake Egyptian antiques made in Birmingham from the real articles, and fake period furniture and art pieces from those that are genuine. Those who are interested can devise quite a number of experiments in this field.

CHAPTER FIVE

# POSTSCRIPT

The writing of this book has been for us a labour of love. Quite apart from any considerations of royalties, we have derived great satisfaction in putting together some of the knowledge concerning this wonderful faculty which we have gained through some fifty-three years of practical experience in the field.

There are few books on the subject, and what there are seem mostly to be written from a sectarian, religious point of view. We have tried in this book to avoid any such approach, since we firmly believe, as we have suggested in the body of the book, that these psychic faculties are in themselves in the same category as our other physical plane senses, and do not depend upon our moral or ethical outlook.

At the same time, of course, it will have become evident to those who have read so far, that there is a definite standard which must be maintained by the would-be psychometrist.

This does not mean that a psychometrist must belong to any definite religious body, but it does mean that if he is to get the full value out of his work, he must be prepared to discipline himself.

The Bible says, 'greater is he that controlleth himself than he that taketh a city by arms'. This self-control is one of the greatest virtues of the psychometrist, and must, if it is to be really effective, extend over a wide area of his own personal self, and become a powerful factor in his everyday life.

Having more control over himself, the psychometrist finds that he is beginning to have more power over others, and at once certain ethical considerations come into play.

## Rules of Conduct

Since he finds himself able to exert power over others around him, he is now faced with the question, what kind of influence are you going to exert on others, and by what authority do you use this influence? There is a saying that power corrupts, and certainly in this field of psychic activity the temptations of power arise, and the more successful in his work the psychic becomes, the greater is the temptation to misuse his power over others.

All the discipline which he has imposed upon himself so far is an emotional and mental control, and it is this discipline which gives him his power. But how shall that power be employed, what rules shall he follow, and what code of conduct shall he apply to himself? All these are questions which he must ask himself before he goes any further in his work.

We have carefully avoided any sectarian, religious approach to this purely natural faculty, but now we are compelled to enter the field of religion, for the exercise of these powers, as of every power we possess, is in essence a spiritual thing. There can be no dichotomy; no splitting of life into 'spiritual' and 'material', for all existence is in the last resort a spiritual thing.

## Teachings of Religion

So we may look for some code of conduct, some rules to follow in the teachings of religion. This is, of course, the age of iconoclasm, the breaking down of all old established images and, of course, the enthronement of new images, for man must have *some* images, some rules. The old codes are therefore out of favour, but we are going to suggest that they may yet return to power.

In the early days of the Russian Revolution the idea of permissiveness which seems to be the keynote of today was extended to the whole area of sexual ethics, and the 'free love' which is being so fervently advocated by many people today was allowed to flourish.

However, the resulting misery and the social disruption consequent upon the application of the free love ethic was such that the Russian rulers revoked this permissiveness and moved back towards the very image which they had in their haste cast down.

## The Ten Commandments

We would suggest, therefore, that the code of conduct known as the Ten Commandments is a useful one for anyone who is using these extended powers of the self. The summary of the law, as given by Jesus, is a positive affirmation of this same code, but in the present state of semantic chaos, when the meanings of words seem to be in doubt, perhaps the definite and blunt statements of the old Mosaic code may be more helpful.

Other religions have their own ethical codes, and such can be of value to the developing psychic. For ourselves, we long ago took the standards laid down by the Master Jesus as our code of conduct, and though on many occasions we must own to having transgressed that code, yet it remains as a guiding line in the difficulties of life, and particularly in the difficulties which arise in the exercise of these supernormal powers of the mind.

Our final word to our readers is, adopt a standard, impose upon yourself a system of self-discipline and then go forward with the development of this power. So will it bring to you, as it has brought to us over the years, happiness and increased opportunities of serving your fellow man.

For in the end, the sole reason for any intensive cultivation of this or any other faculty is, in the words of the neophyte who stands before the door of the Lodge of the Mysteries, 'I desire to know, in order to serve', and that service is to God and his fellow men, and brings some glimpse of that true peace and freedom which come from One who said, 'I am amongst you as one who serves'. For indeed as Dante said, long ago, 'In His Will is our peace'.